Anthology of Ohio Poets

by Tina Toles
and the
West-Dayton Christian Writers
Guild, Inc.

WinePress Publishing
MUKILTEO, WA 98275

Anthology of Ohio Poets
Copyright © 1997 by Tina Toles

Published by WinePress Publishing
PO Box 1406, Mukilteo, WA 98275

All scripture quotations are taken from the King James Version of the Bible. Copyright © 1979,1980,1982 Thomas Nelson Inc., Publishers.

Printed in the United States of America
Library of Congress Catalog Card Number: 96-61547
ISBN 1-883893-54-2

Dedication

This book is dedicated in loving memory of the following individuals:

LaShawnda Reese	March 20, 1970–Feb. 16, 1976
Leo Wilson	June 27, 1899–Sept. 5, 1980
James N. Payne Sr.	Dec. 28, 1918–Sept. 28, 1988
Harold V. Harrington	March 31, 1929–June 3, 1989
Charles D. Henderson	Jan. 29.1928–Nov.4, 1991
Randolph Sills, Jr.	April 20, 1935–May 10, 1993
Stanley A. Reese Jr.	April 24, 1918–April 22, 1994
William T. Head	May 13, 1951–Sept. 17, 1994
Frank Value Sr.	April 9, 1926–July 29, 1995
Jackie Davis	April 23, 1963–Nov. 21, 1995
David J. Tellis	June 17, 1972–Dec. 15, 1995
Inez Phelps	April 28, 1914–Feb. 14, 1995
Mary L. Moore	Sept. 3, 1909–Nov. 5, 1995
Othello Kelley	Oct. 23, 1915–Sept. 27, 1995
Charles D. Henderson Jr.	Nov. 8, 1974–Jan. 24, 1996
Mary Brumfield	Aug. 3, 1907–Aug. 16, 1996
Charles Underwood	Jan. 2, 1919–Feb. 26, 1996

"My Mother's Grandfather Clock" is dedicated to the
memory of Mrs. Mamie Adeline Werr Jackson
March 24, 1885–December 31, 1994

West-Dayton Christian Writers Guild Inc.

The West-Dayton Christian Writers Guild was organized in December, 1993. It is a non-profit and tax-exempt organization. Mrs. Tina V. Toles is the Founder/President. The Writers' Guild is a support group for novice and professional writers. Our objective is to support those who feel called by God to develop their God given talents. To support individuals who want to grow spiritually and develop their writing skills. The Writers Guild provides inspiration to those who write for the Glory of God. The Writers' Guild goal is to minister throughour writing. We write to become better stewards of Gods' gift. Our mission is to educate, train and encourage others to write. To write as a means of preserving history, for the next generation. To leave a legacy for all to see and read. We offer current Writers market information. We have a monthly guest speaker. Yearly, we hold a mini-workshop which consist of Poets and Authors from various cities and states. We invite you to become a member of the Writers' Guild. We meet at the Madden Hills Library, 2542 Germantown Pike, Dayton, Ohio 45408, We meet the second Saturday of each month, from 2:00-4:00 P.M. Please come join us.

Mrs. Tina Toles, Founder/President
West-Dayton Chistian Writers Guild Inc.

Writing For Gods' Glory
Hebrews 13:21

West-Dayton Christian Writers Guild Inc.

Membership Roster

Tina Toles
Doug Toles
Debra Wagner
Melvin Jackson
Patricia Behnken
Bernice Tippit
Wealtha Yarbrough
Verlena Hawkins
Frances Moore
Benette DeCoux
Nozipo Glenn
Annie Turner
Howard Ross
Linda Jordan
Lena Arnold
Toni Ewu
Annie King
Olivia Harris
Cinde Williams

Corena Johnson
Mary Martin
Joan Lindsey
Rosa Smith
Linda Shaw
Patricia Lewis
Mary Watts
Elaine Saffold
Granada Kendrick
Elizabeth Russell
Frankie Garrison
Irene Bullet
Beverly Tevis
Robin Johnson
Jackie Mckenize
Ordell Jones
Irene Garrett
Mike Johnson
Bea Bolton

William Diggs
Rose Wilson
Sarah Tims
Gloria White
Flonzie B. Wright (Honorary)
Anna Taylor-Clark
Bernadette Harawa
Robert Abernathy
Marsha Lewis
Odell Cox

Willa Powell
Robert Lewis
Clarence Norton
Lillya Branham

Henry Joseph
Beatrice Abernathy
Barbara Davis
Leonard Dean
Larry Blair

Special Thanks

Special thanks to the members of the West-Dayton Christian Writers Guild, for your encouragement, support and assistance in this endeavor. Without you the Anthology would not be possible. You have been a blessing to me. This Anthology was written in hopes of giving our members and other Poets in Ohio who have never published, because of a lack of funds and or a lack of knowledge an opportunity to be published. This is a fulfillment of a dream. To create a special collection of poems that would be inspirational and motivational. We have been writing for Gods' Glory and He has blessed the Writers Guild. The contents of this volume expresses the varied views and talents of our writers. I hope this Anthology will encourage others to use their God given talents for His glory. It's truly a source of great satisfaction and very rewarding.

Christian Writers Guilds

Special Thanks to the following Christian Writers' Guilds for their support and encouragement given to the West-Dayton Christian Writers' Guild Inc.

Columbus Christian Writers'
Columbus, Ohio
Mrs. Brenda Custodio
614-861-1011

Dayton Christian Scribes
Kettering, Ohio
Mrs. Lois Peece
513-433-6470

Greater Cincinnati Christian Writers'
Cincinnati, Ohio
Mrs. Theresa Cleary
513-521-1913

Western Ohio Christian Writers'
Sidney, Ohio
Mrs. Alice Linsley
513-663-4131

Yellow Spings Writers' Group
Yellow Springs, Ohio
Mrs. Sandra Love
513-767-9112

Financial Contribution Statement

The West-Dayton Christian Writers Guild Inc. Is a non-profit and tax-exempt organization. (Under 1702 of the Ohio Revised Code) Internal Revenue Code (501(a) (501(c)-3
The Writers Guild needs your financial contributions and support if we are to thrive and flourish. If you wish to make a donation to the Writers Guild, any and all contributions are tax deductible. Upon request we will supply you with our tax exempt number. We thank you in advance for your encouragement and support. Without you our dreams could not become a reality.

All funds derived from the sale of the Anthology of Ohio Poets will be donated to the West-Dayton Christian Writers to aid and assist in their endeavors.

Disclaimer

The West Dayton Christian Writers Guild has been given permission to publish and reproduce the following material. All authors that have submitted poems, have assured the Writers Guild that the poems are original. Not having any reasons to believe anything to the contrary the poems have been published. Therefore the Writers Guild is not and will not be responsible, for acts of copyright infringement or plagiarism. All copyrights are retained by the individual authors. No material in this book may be reproduced in any form without written permission from its author. If there are any questions regarding any poems included within this Anthology, questions should be directed to the author.

Table Of Contents

Tina Toles

Mary Watts

Debra Wagner

Discover the excitement of knowing and serving the King of Glory through the creative expressions of the these talented writers. This book of poetry and prose is designed for personal reading, pleasure and profit in daily reflection. Read with deliverance and joy!

Terrence K. Grimes
Minister of Music
Shiloh Missionary Baptist Church

Foreword

The manifestation of the West-Dayton Christian Writers Guild is truly God sent, I believe. We praise and thank God for the inspiration He gave this vivacious Founder/President Tina Toles and these wonderful cooperative members to rise up and leave a legacy in order that generations to come will know that we passed this way. These are Christian men and women, boys and girls. Stirring up their God given gifts and talents for the Masters use.

Tina Toles the Founder/President is bless with diversity of gifts, but her gift is love, yes love for God and love for her fellowman. She encourages saints everywhere to exercise their God given writing ability. These saints are writing for God's glory. Each one having his or her own expression of God's love in poetry and books. The dichotomy of the uniqueness and the glorious strength in togetherness is an important plus for the Writers Guild. For in togetherness there is strength, encouragement, edification and power saturated in love. What then can we say, knowing they are writing for God's glory, using God's gift, His wisdom and power. Success is theirs for the claiming. We are rejoicing with you, seeing that you are rooted and grounded in God's *word*, utilizing His *wisdom* to do His will, His way. May God bless and keep you is my prayer.

Sis. Irene M. Ford, Owner
Peace Christian Bookstore
Dayton, Ohio

Tina Toles, Author/ Founder/President
West-Dayton Christian Writers Guild Inc.

Take Inventory

If Christ called you home today
Would you be ready to go
If He ask you of your deeds
What would you have to say
Have you lived a Christian life
Have you witnessed to anyone today
About His goodness and His mercy
Have you brought anyone to Christ
Have you kept His Ten Commandments
Is your life in order
Take Inventory of your works
For the victory is at hand
"Therefore my beloved brethren Be ye
Steadfast Unmoveable always abounding
In the works of the Lord"   1 Corinthians 15:58
Forasmuch as ye know that your labor is not in vain in the Lord".

We Take For Granted

We take for granted the five senses given by God
The simple movement of our bodies
We take for granted the beauty of a rose
Never stopping along the way to smell or touch
We take for granted those small words of affection
"I love you"
What's saddest of all
We take each other for granted
We take for granted
That when we close our eyes at night
We'll live to see another day
Many words are left unspoken
We take for granted so many things
So before it's too late
Take time to appreciate the simple things in life
Stop putting off for another time, another day
Because tomorrow may never come

I'm A Soldier

I'm a soldier in the army, of the Lord
I volunteered for this army
I ask the Lord to use me
To lead and guide me on this pathway, I've chosen to travel
I'm a warrior fighting against satan
Fighting against the strong holds of sin
And the lust of flesh
I'm a warrior in God's army
A battle that I must fight, a battle that can't be lost
For the Lord is on my side
I'm ready, willing and able
I've put on the full armor of God
I'm saving soul's for Christ and the victory is at hand
The devil's been defeated
Won't you help me spread the word
I invited you to join this army
For with this invitation, comes the promise of eternal life
This is my reward and it can be yours, too
There's a job in my God's army, He's waiting for you
Can't you see Him, standing there
With arms stretched wide open
Let me reassure you, that you won't, that you can't be denied
When you accept Him as your Savior
You need only to apply

Turn It Over

So you say you are a Christian
That you believe in God
You know what ever happens, is only the Master's plan
But when you had a problem
To Him you didn't turn
You tried to solve the problem
You worried and you cried, no sleep or peace of mind
But when you couldn't solve it
You remembered gramma's words

"That prayer changes things"
If only you'd remember, to call upon His name
Then to Him, you turned in prayer
You left it at the altar, you left it there for awhile
Then picked it up again
One more try, you said to yourself
I'm sure I can fix it
But of course you couldn't fix it
Weary, worn and defeated
 You turned it over to Him again
Of course the Lord will fix it
If you stay out the way
Let the Lord have His way
In His on time, and in His own way
He'll fix it

Give Me My Roses

I'm tried and I'm weary
This old body don't move the way it used to
The hair on my head, has turned gray
My mind don't work the way it should
So if you love me
Take time to give me roses
While I can still see their beauty
And smell their lovely fragrance
For when this old body is laid to rest
The flowers sent for me I shall not see
I shall not see their beauty
Or smell their lovely fragrance
The tears you shed I shall not see hear
The final parting words of affection
"I love you"
Will not be heard by me
So while the blood flows freely
And this old body is still warm
Take time to say I love you

Take time to shower me with tokens of affection
For when my body lies before you
And I have passed through those pearly gates
Time for us will be no more

You Need Jesus

You need Jesus in your life
Maybe you don't know it now
Because no one has told you, of His goodness of His grace
But just keep on living
Times will get tough, your night will be long
Some tears you will shed
Friends will turn their back on you
They will cause you great pain
Family and loved ones you won't be able to find
But I can tell you for sure, who will be there
Jesus will be there
Waiting with open arms
He is the answer, to all your problems
You need Jesus in your life
He will be there when you need Him
No matter what the problem
He's never to busy
He's never unavailable
Now you know, that you need Jesus in your life
You need Jesus in your life, because
He's the way the truth and the light
And He's your Savior

Be Still

Be still God is speaking to you
Be still and listen
He wants to speak to you
He has a job for you to do

Be still
How can you hear if you don't listen
If you aren't still you may miss your blessing
Be still and know that He is God
He has a job for you to do
A very special job
One that only you can do
You won't know what to do, if you don't listen
He has a message for you and only you
He is speaking to you
Be still and let Him have His way
He is preparing you
He wants to use you in His service
You may not understand it now
But just be patient and you will see
You have been chosen
The choice is yours
He's calling you
Because there's work for you to do
Be still let Him show you the way
He wants to lead and guide you
If only you will surrender
To His will and to His way
Listen He's speaking

Broken Hearted

Oh God, I feel brokenhearted
I've lost my will and reason to live
So much pain
It seems much easier to just lay down and die
Because I can't bear the pain
You've taken my only child
I know, I'm not surpose to question your will
But oh' God, I just don't understand, Why
He was taken at such a young age
He had so much love to give and still so much to accomplish
He was a good child and he did nothing wrong

But yet you took him away from me
So now, I ask you Dear God, help me to accept your will
Ease my pain, Lord, touch my heart
Stop the pain, stop the tears
Give me a reason for living
Strengthen me and strengthen my faith
Restore my joy, restore my peace
I believe in you, Lord
Fix me Jesus, make things alright
I need you to fix me, as only you can
I want to be able to smile and laugh again
Give me understanding
I have heard it said
Things happen for a reason
Help me learn from this tragedy
Teach me Lord, thy will
So that I may be able to help others
That feel brokenhearted and alone
To help, other Mothers understand
That I surived and you can too
You may not know it now, because the pain is so great
But, God loves you and so do I

Lord I'm Willing

Oh' Lord I'm willing to do your will
Use me Lord
To sing your praises, to speak your words
Teach me thy will, not mine, but thy will be done
If my family and friends won't go, I will
I want to be a witness for thee
Use me, use me as you see fit
Show me thy will
I'm your child and I love you Lord
I'm willing to do your will
Willing to walk this christian journey
Lord, here am I willing to do your will
Willing to put on the whole armor of God

To fight a war against satan
Because satan is a lier
He comes to steal our joy and our souls
Willing to do your will
Willing to follow your commandments
 "Thy shalt have no other God before Me"
Willing to do His will
Willing to serve thee until I die
Willing to witness to others, about His love and plan of Salvation
Willing to do your will
Willing to read the Bible and study your word
I'm willing, ready and able to do your will

His Promise

Sometimes my path seems dark and dreary
Oh Lord, I need you
I need you to be a light unto my pathway
To guide and direct me
As I travel this Christian journey
You see, I thought this journey would be easy
But it's not easy
He never promised, it would be
In His word He promised Eternal Life
If I lived a christian life
He never promised
I wouldn't have burdens to bare
Or tears to shed
In His word, He did promise
To never leave me alone
He promised to comfort me in times of sorrows
He promised to wipe away the tears and calm my fears
He promised eternal peace
If I labor in His vineyard
The path I have choosen will not be easy
In fact, because I'm a christian
I have been persecuted, lied on
Mistreated and abused

But I must remember God's promises
Of joy, peace and happiness in His Kingdom
Trials and tribulations will all be over
No more sickess, No more sorrow, No more pain
As I travel this Christian journey
I must remember
"The race isn't given to swift, but to those who endure to the
end"

It's A Blessing

Have you stopped to count your blessing
Have you thought about how blessed you are
Stop for a moment to think about how truly blessed you are
We take so many things for granted
The good Lord is blessing you each day of your life
But we're so busy living life to it's fullest
We can't or don't take the time to say, Thank You Lord
It's a blessing to know God loves you
It's a blessing to know He cares for you
It's a blessing to fill His Holy Spirit
His peace and His joy
Oh' what a wonderful feeling to know that God love's us so
That He gave His only begotten son
That we might have the right to eternal life
It's a blessing to have complete inner peace
To wake up to a brand new day
It's a blessing
No more worries
No more fears
Don't waste another moment, another second
Give thanks to the Master, from whom all blessing flows

Prayer

When I learned to pray, It changed my life
Things began to happen
When I learned how to communicate with God
It changed my whole life
I don't mean a prayer of "Now I lay me down to sleep"
I don't mean the Lord's Prayer
I'm talking about a personal prayer
A down to earth, real prayer from the bottom of my heart
I prayed and my prayers were answered
Prayer changed my life
I'm a witness prayer changes things
Prayer really works
You need Jesus in your life
You need to have a personal relationship with Him
 There's such inner peace, joy and happiness
I can feel His holy spirit, moving in me
I searched for Him, and I found Him
He's not hard to find
You need only to accept Him
Accept Him as your Saviour
He loves you and He wants your love
Pray to Him
Ask Him to lead and guide you
Prayer is the key, prayer changes things

Author, Mary Lue Watts
Mt. Olive Baptist Church
Rev. Theodore MacFarlane Jr., Pastor

Dressed For Battle In God's Army

Build up your strength in union with God
By means of His mighty power, God will never leave you
He will be with you everyday and everyhour
Put on the armor that God has given to you
With the armor of God, you will surely make it through
You will be able to stand against the devil's evil tricks
For he is hiding around every corner
And even under the little bricks
You know, we are not fighting against just human beings
But we are fighting against bodies unseen
We are fighting against spiritual wickedness in high places
Against the rulers
Authorities and cosmic powers with hidden faces
Use every piece of God's armor
To resist the enemy when he attacks
And when the battle is over
You will be standing firm in your tracks
Be ready with truth as a belt fitting tightly around your waist
And the breastplate of righteousness in just the right place
Wear the shoes that are prepared
With the gospel of peace upon your feet
Then go and spread the good news of Jesus to everyone you meet
Above all you will need to take faith as your shield
So when the burning arrows are shot by the wicked one
To satan you will not yield
Put on the helmet of salvation as protection for your head
God gave His only begotten Son to save us from our sins
Now you will need the sword of the spirit
Which is the Word of God
Using a two edge sword cutting sin left
And right which seems so very hard
Do all of this in prayer, asking God for the help you need
Keeping alert and never giving up, praying on every occasion
As the Spirit leads
When the battle is over and you have done your best
Then God will say come on home my child and take your rest
Then you can say, I have fought a good fight

The day is over and long gone the night
I have finished my work down here on earth
Now I'm going on up to heaven to that eternal place
Up in heaven a crown of righteousness is waiting for me
And I will live with Jesus for eternity!

Door Keeper In The House Of The Lord

Ushers are doorkeepers in the house of the Lord
We do our best to keep the people on one accord
There are Ushers standing at the door
To direct the people to the Ushers standing on the floor
Some are in the middle aisle and some are along the wall
We are here to give a hardy welcome to one and all
So come on into my Father's House
Join us in worship and enjoy yourself, oh so very much
We help to put the congregation in the right frame of mind
So they can receive the Pastor's message and not be left behind
We meet the people with a smile and a warm hello too
When they look downhearted we know just what to do
When we show you to your seat
There on the pew some more of God's people you will meet
Now, to the members sitting on the pew
Just remember the whole seat doesn't belong to you
So when the Usher with a smile, sit someone next to you
Please step out in the middle aisle and let them through
I know some of you like the end seat
When the service is over, out the door the others you will beat
Members, if by chance you are not on time
Don't look at the person seated, as to say, "This seat is mine".
We as Ushers have a job to do
As much as we try we can't please all of you
Come on everybody, let us sing praises to the Lord with a shout
Let us set this house on Holy Ghost fire and keep the devil out

Building A Winning Team

B - is for Bible, God's written Holy word
U - is for Understanding, why God loves even the little bird
I - is for Investment, that God made in you and me
L - is for Love, God loved us so much that He gave
His only begotten son to die on Calvary
D - is for Dedication, to Christ we will forever give
I - is for Immanuel, we know that God is with us forever
N - is for Never, Jesus will never forsake you, or leave you alone
G - is for Grace, God's grace is sufficient to keep us when we feel
all hope is gone
A - is for Answer, God will hear and answer your prayer
W - is for Wonderful, Jesus is a wonderful friend who is by your
side no matter when or where
I - is for Inspiration, with inspiration from God,
man was moved to write His message for all to read
N - is for News, the angel brought the good news to the three
wisemen
I - is for Immaculate, for Jesus was born of a virgin,
an immaculate birth
G - is for Greatest, the greatest story that was ever told was of
Jesus and His undying love
T - is for Trust, if you trust in God with all of your heart and
Soul, you will live forever in heaven above
E - is for Everyone, with everyone working together with the
Holy Sprit as our guide we claim the victory
A - is for Attitude, our attitude will be a contributing factor in
determining this reality
M - is for Meditation. With much meditation and prayer I bring
this title to you hoping that something has been said that will
help you on your journey through

When I Can't Take Care Of You Anymore

When I can't take care of you anymore
Deep in my heart I know that I must let you go
Something came up and I had to leave you in someone else's care

I thought you would be lonely if I left you there
When I said to you that I was ready to go
I thought you would be the first one to the door
Out of your seat you did not rise
Instead you kept talking to the people who were sitting there
And I knew that I was leaving you with someone who really cared
Still deep down in my heart I felt a little sad
These are feelings that you may not understand
How proud I am to see my baby growing into a man
Progress sometimes, seems so very slow
But with lots of love and patience I can still see him growing
When I reached my destination, I called just to say hello
He answered and said, "sorry mom, but I've got to go."
I hung up the phone with mixed emotions
Knowing within myself this was like a promotion
This young man who has been with me all of his life
Has finally stayed away from home, without any strife
My son is growing up and leaving me behind
But he will always be my baby, and he's always on my mind
I realize that I am getting older everyday
And at home with me, my son can not always stay
I love this special child, this is true
And when the time comes to give him up
I'm not sure what I'll do
Now, to all of you parents who feel the way I do
Just leave it to the Master and He will see you through
I know there is a God who looks after us all
He will always be there to catch you just before you fall

He Died For Me

They hung my Lord on that old rugged cross
Where He shed His blood for all the lost
They whipped Him up Calvary's Hill
While the people stood silent and still
They pierced Him in the side
Their on that old rugged cross He hung His head and died
He died for you, He died for me
That we might have life eternally
They buried Him in Joseph's tomb
Not knowing that He would rise, early Sunday morning
Jesus rose on Easter morn
His Blood He shed to wash our sins away
He rose from the dead early Sunday morning
The scars from the crown, still on His head
With the nail prints still in His hands
Today we celebrate His resurrection
And the gift He promised of eternal life

35

Author, Debra Wagner
Dixion United Methodist Church
Rev. Warren Hill, Pastor

God What Is My Task

God what is my task, how will I know
I cannot Sing
I cannot Preach
I am not a Teacher
I am nothing, I think
My sister says "God will let you know, not to worry
He will tell you
My brother says "Keep the faith
God is good, God is great
When the time is right
God will tell you, what your task in life is to be
Both have said, keep on searching
Keep doing His will, God is with you
You will see, God will show you, It will be
I believe in God, I know He looks after me
I know my task will be one, He has set aside especially for me
Until that time I shall wonder
God, what is my task

Love, Life, Everlasting

Love, life, everlasting
What do those words mean to me
Who loved us so much
He gave His Son's life
So that we may be everlasting free
Love, life, everlasting
What do those words mean to me
Love, Life, everlasting
Is this what God has in mind for me
Love, life, everlasting
Is this what will be
Love, life, everlasting
Is this the path I want for me

My Life

Sometime I feel as if I don't have a friend
As if my world is going to end
Sometimes I feel like I can't go on
As if I'm in this world all alone
I do my best to do what's right
But still I feel I'm loosing the fight
How do I win
How do I survive
When no man seems to be on my side
Well, as I was taught when you're loosing the fight
Lean on God
Trust in Him
God will be your strongest friend
God will aid you
God is your solace in these trying times

Did You Know

Did you know, Blacks and Whites will one day unite
Did you know, there will be no anger and strife
Did you know, time will end
Did you know, there will be no more sin
Did you know, He died to save our souls
Did you know, He will rise again
Did you know or didn't you care
God will save us
This will be His sweet, sweet end!

Sonnet

I write this sonnet because I long to be free
I write this sonnet because it sings to me
I write this sonnet to tell you a fable
Of a lady oppressed, trying to do her best
Oppressed by the freedoms her life can barely afford
Oppressed by the feelings her man chooses to ignore
Oppressed by the standards society inflicts
Oppressed by a mind set she has yet to lick
I write this sonnet to express her grief
Grief that her children still aren't free
Grief that her mind can't bear anymore
Grief that her burdens are too large to ignore
Grief that her life will soon be through
And that her life made no difference, based on what she could do
I write this sonnet, because her spirit has no peace
I write this sonnet, because I understand her need
I write this sonnet, because she never gave up the fight
I write this sonnet, because her spirit cries out to be heard

Author, Verlena D. Hawkins
Marathana Fellowship Church
Rev. Turman Martin, Pastor

Don't Think God Doesn't Care

When your pain gets so intense
Unable for you to bear
Don't think that God has forgotten you
And that He doesn't care
For He knew about this pain filled day
Before the foundation of the earth
He knew about your situation before your birth
Stand on God's word and be obedient
Because He cares
Even in your time of weeping
He hears your heart's prayer
He still calls forth for you to be strong
And for you to be courageous
In the mist of this heated battle and as the storm rages
He does cares for you, His Child
No matter what God choose
Concerning the pain you must bear
Don't ever think He doesn't Love you
Don't ever think God doesn't care

Always In My Hands

Lord, I don't know what in the world is happening to me
My life is spinning out of control
I can no longer see your face
I feel so lonely and abandoned, because my loved ones are gone
I can't feel your presence, I just feel so all alone
I feel the tugging and spinning
The spinning of a wheel
Things have become so quickly confused
Life no longer feels real
Tears have begun to suddenly overflow, when no one is present
My very soul is weary, for my spirit has been cast down
But then I heard your loving voice
As you came to see about me, He said,
"I am the potter, you are the clay"

I'm making you as you ought to be
I took you and placed you on the potter's wheel
Through your life, circumstances seem to spin out of control
But you were always in My divine hands and I had a firm hold
Your tears represented the water and the washing by My word
Which I spoke to you so convincingly and which you always heard
In all of that twirling and spinning
My foot controlled the pedal
I was making you firm and sure, I was making you settle
I never pressed your soul down, I always pulled you up
Life seemed so terribly unbearable
As you drank from it's bitter cup
You were so frustrated, because you didn't understand
That through all of that spinning, you were always in My hands

Happy Mother's Day, Mom

As I think of you this Mother's Day
I want to tell you in my own way
How much I appreciate your time and tears
Trying to cultivate character
Through these many years
The patience you gave me
When no one else understood
Training me to grow up like I should
Investing so much time, in little old me
You knew things then, that I could not see
So many things you tried diligently to teach
Having my own ideas, you could not reach me
Being stubborn I felt I knew it all
Neglecting everything
I was off to a ball game
But today things make more sense to me
As I am becoming what you wanted me to be
A spiritual woman, mature, serene and complete
A daughter just like her Mother
Happy Mother's Day

You Were Always There

You were always there just for little old lonely me
Helping me to be the very best that I could ever be
There were many times when I really didn't understand
That your way of showing love was lending a helping hand
We had many hard times but with love we made it through
And today, my dear friend, I want to show you
How much I appreciate you
You were always there with a kind word and a lovely smile
Not realizing that ministering to me might take awhile
But somehow that never really bothered or even concerned you
You realized that you had a special and important job to do
That job was to help me and bring me to this end
And because of your hard work, you grew to be my friend
You were always there for me and now I'm there for you
To love, encourage and see you through
Making your day a little more sweeter and a little bit brighter
Helping you carry your burdens and to make your load lighter
I want you to know with all my heart that I really care
And I'm here for you today
Because yesterday you were always there for me

Memorial To You Mom

Dear Mom how clearly I remember the day you went away
All the things that you had done and the things you had to say
The last moments with you I'll cherish you for the rest of my life
Those moments have comforted me through all of the strife
I choose to remember the good times that you have given me
So full and free
Your godly living
Still has an impact upon me
Thank you for sharing with me about Jesus
Whom I acknowledge as the Christ
And all that He has done for me
By paying the sacrifical price

I have continued in my faith with Him
Which you had taught me from a child
I have grown so much in Him
Even though it took me awhile
As many years have come and gone
My heart has learned to be calm
My obedience to the Lord Jesus
Is my memorial to you Mom

Author, Linda Jordan
Englewood Assemble Church Of God and Christ
Rev. Dan Crabtree, Pastor

A Touch Of God's Love

As the Sun is rising, and the day begins
Let us make this a special day
Looking at the world in a new way
As we give Praise unto the Lord
For this special day
As the Suns' light shines over our face
We can feel a warm touch of Gods' love and grace
As He takes time to assure us in His special way
That He cares about everything we do even this day
He will see us through

Proven Love

His love is still shining through
His blood is still providing the way to life abundantly
If it had not been for the old rugged cross
Where His love showed, and His blood flowed
To redeem the lost
We could have never known, the strength of His love
Which still carries us through
Mountains we face and strong holds that rise
Temptation tries to lead me in a direction
God has shown us to be wrong
That life will not stand
Death shall overtake us
It's not Gods' will, but the leading of deceit
Sorrows we'll face, for there is no honor in deceit
Only God holds Honor

The Trinity

Father, Son, Holy Spirit three in one
Alpha and Omega, the beginning and the end
Spring forth spiritual waters
Filling us with your love
As we learn of your ways
Delivering us from temptation
Sent to destroy our life in you
Lead us through green pastures
Helping us to overcome trials and tribulations
Open our eyes that we may see your ways, and not ours
Allow us to hear your voice not the enemy
Make our burdens light as you mend our lives

The Victorious One

As He walked through the sand
They proudly stood among Him
Degrading our Lord and Savior
Their words harshly, angerly racing in the air
On the cross baring sin and shame
He would carry it through the streets
As they approached that day
The angry crowd stood among Him
So proud of themselves on that day
As nails begin to reign out, piercing our Lord and Saviors hands
Laughter, mockery, reign out with words of hatred
Crucify Him, kill Him
Not believing He would return
As He hung there in the sun
Darkness began to over take, as His Father turned away
Death suddenly appeared, it was finished

In the garden, Jesus spoke unto Peter and said
Thou shalt deny me thrice
Three nails were driven into Christ, our Lord and Savior
The redeemer of man from sin
One bright morning, three days later
God visited the tomb
An Abundance of light, the Holy Spirit filled the tomb
On the outside Angels stood
As the Holy presence of our heavenly Father appeared with power
Strength, Love, Joy and peace then came forth, Jesus
Gods' Holy Son, the redeemer of men

Enlighten Your Children

Come Oh Lord, enlighten us unto your truth
Open our minds to your Word
As you illuminate your truth
Enter into our hearts
Give us, love, peace, joy that's beyond our understanding
Allow your love to flow through us
As living waters unto the thirsty
Anoint us with your oil
To reach the thirsty in dry deserts
Be in the midst of us
Fill us with your Holy presence
Pour through us your spirit
To unlock the doors that have been closed by rejection
Oh God be in the midst
And grant our prayers this day
For unto you shall all the honor and glory
Be given each day

Author, Corena Johnson
Hillcrest S.D.A. Church
Rev. Wayne Mcknight, Pastor

The Master Plan

Can't you hear the message
The Lord is speaking to you
He's telling us to get ready
Because He's coming soon
The warning signs have told us
But you're too blind to see
Remember the days of Noah
The people that did not believe
He is giving you a chance to get ready
So you better take heed
It's now time for the master plan to begin
Wars are no longer rumors
Famines have spread throughout our lands
The starving people of this world will no longer suffer and grieve
Kings throughout our nations will have to give up their thrones
Our King of Kings is coming back
So we can live in peace and harmony
So please stop, look and listen
The Lord delivered His message in hopes of bringing
His people together for a life, until eternity
Repent, watch and pray
The master plan has began

A Prayer Of Innocence

Lord, teach me how to pray
I try so hard, but I can't seem to find the right words
Lord, I put my trust in you
I know of your great blessings
For you have bestowed on me many blessings
You brought me through many things
My health, strength and sanity
With all the stress now in this world
I know my strength is coming from above
If these words don't seem right

Forgive me Lord!
You know these words are coming from my heart
When we start to get old
Our memory seems to come and go
Lord, I know you've answered me
For I can feel that inner peace
I know you are my best friend
Because you told me
You would be here until the end

Yesterday

Yesterday has come and gone
It's a past memory that lingers on
Some of our yesterday's were lonely
Some were very pleasant and some were sad
But life goes on
So let's concentrate on living today
As long as it shall last
Yesterday is a memory
Tomorrow is a dream
The future may or may not be
Only God knows our present, future and our past
Today is the day to thank God
For every breath we take

No More Rules

I remember the days of old
When children were children
They did what they were told
There were rules to follow day by day
Seldom did they have to be scolded
They ran errands and tended the chores
Never complained if asked to do more

Many things have changed
As the years go by
Children no longer have rules to abide by
Lord, teach them to pray
For only you can keep them from going astray
Proverbs 4-1 Hear, ye children, the instruction of a father
And attend to know understanding.

Going Home

I have stayed with you long enough
Now it's time to relieve the pressure
From each and everyone of you
My body has gone through much more pain
Than God wanted me to endure
So please don't waste any more unnecessary tears
I'm ready to go home
Rejoice with me
God has taken my soul to His eternal resting place
Be happy for me and thank Him
He has released me from thid terrible excruciating pain
Only God knows just how much we can bear
Always remember that I loved each
And everyone of you with all my heart
My mind is at peace now
I'm ready to go home
Promise me that you will get your life in order
And that you'll share, this eternal peace with me in Christ
I'm going home

Author, Bernice Tippit
Collegiate Heights Church of God and Christ
Rev. John Smalley, Pastor

Make Me Worthy

Make me worthy of your many blessings
Oh, God, sometimes I don't realize just how many blessings
I receive daily, from being in your care
You are so merciful and kind to me
Bless your sweet name
Hallelujah
You are so great
Dear God, thank you for letting the blood
Still run warm in my veins
Bless your Holy name
Hallelujah
Thank you, thank you, for letting me breath
Think, and move my body
I must say how great you are
I can't praise you enough
Please, accept my humble thanks for everything you do

Our God Is Real

If you don't believe there is a God
Try breathing on your own
Can you move a muscle without God giving you the strength
All your thinking ability comes from God
Your eyesight and all your body movements
Are possible only if it's God's will they move
Never doubt for a moment that there is a supreme being
The moon, the sun and the stars are all made by God
Our bodies were created by Him
Everything is so modern
So modern that some people think we were created by accident
I hope your common sense
Serves you well enough to accept the fact that God does exist
Have you tried waking up in the morning or any other time
Without God, it's impossible, isn't it
He is everything to us
God is real and He is alive

Thank You Jesus

Thank you Jesus, for another day and another night
We are so thankful for the many blessings
That thou hast bestowed upon us
Bless the poor, sick and afflicted
Bless the widows and the orphans
Have mercy on the many people in our prisons
For they are forgotten
Please Jesus, look down with an eye of pity
On all the elderly people in rest homes and institutions
Dear Jesus, dear Savior of this world
Bless the poor that have so little and need so much
Give them the understanding
That without You we can do nothing
With you all things are possible
I'm so thankful that you have brought me thus far
I'm weak and tried
If it is Thy will
I beg you for strength to carry on as long as you see fit
I know that you won't put more on us than we can bear
Thanks for helping me to climb one more mountain of this life
Have mercy on all your people
You made us all
You know more about us, then we know about ourselves

Help The Sick And Elderly

Some of the loneliest people in the world
Are people in the nursing homes and hospitals
Can you spend just a few hours or two days a week
Or two days a month doing something to cheer them a little
Maybe you could read to them
They really need to feel loved
Stress and despair has killed more people than any diseases
Sometimes a person is in so much pain they can't pray
We need to try to uplift their spirits

Help them to feel like they are still a part of the human race
And their life is worth living
We must teach them that God cares for them
They have no loved ones to hold them
No one to confide in, not a shoulders to lean on
So if you can give them a hug, a handshake, or a smile
And maybe a little of your time
It would brighten their lives
And you'll feel good knowing you've helped someone

Our Heavenly Father

Dear Father In Heaven

We come to you in the name of your dear son, Jesus
We ask Thy blessing upon our nation
And all our government people
We thank Thee for all the food you have given us today
Be with those who do not have as much as we do
Please comfort and protect them, Lord
Father, we thank Thee and praise Thee for being too wise
To make a mistake, too good to do anything wrong
Too kind and merciful to overlook a person such as I
For You said "I have clothed the flowers of the fields
And the birds of the air, are ye of much more value then these"
We pray that Thy love will cover us as the sky
We ask these things in the wonderful name of Christ Jesus
Our risen Savior

Amen, Amen

Author, Arlene Bullet
Maranatha Christian Church
Rev. Turman Martin, Pastor

He Is Jehovah

I call you friend, He calls you servant
I call you gifted, He calls you anointed
I call you predictable, He calls you prophet
I call you special, He calls you ordained
I call you different, He calls you chosen
I call you legacy, He calls you generation
I call you city, He calls you Israel
I am your neighbor, He is Jehovah, Almighty
The true and living God
I call you weak, He calls you strong
I call you defeated, He calls victorious
I call you timid, He calls you bold
I say surrender, He says fight
I say peace, He says war
For He is Jehovah, strong in battle
For tearing down of strong holds
I call you enemy, He calls you friend
I say die, He says live
I'm your neighbor, He is Jehovah

Of All People

I celebrate Jesus where ever I go
Of all people Jesus stopped by
Filled me with the Holy Ghost
And set me on fire
I wake up singing, dancing
And praising His name
Since Jesus stopped by, I'm not the same
I will forever proclaim His name
Of all people, Jesus stopped by
Believe and never doubt, Jesus is real and so alive
Of all the people Jesus stopped by today

Awake My Soul And Sing

Awake my soul and sing
To welcome the soon and coming King
Awake my soul and sing
Stand, applaud and give honor to the King
Awake my soul and sing
Behold He's adorned in splendor and glory
Awake my soul and sing
For He has lifted me up and set me on high
Forever, will I sing praises to the King
Awake my soul and sing
And welcome the soon and coming King

Far From Free

So you say at last I'm free
But you're bound by sin both in and out
Yet you boast you're free
You poor old wretched soul
Little do you know, you can't be free
Until you bow down on bended knees
Cry out and say yes, to your Lord and Savior
Repent and then you will be free
Oh, how my heart does grieve, for you have been deceived
Try my Lord today, in Him there is no deceit
He really wants you free, don't you hear my plead
Oh my friend confess your sins and rid yourself of them today
My Lord is listening, He's that kind of friend
He truly wants you free
The day will come when you will cry
And yes repent
My God will be listening

Jesus Set Me Free

Drugs, cocaine, money and fame
These are the things that rule our land
Racism runs rapid in this land
These are the things satan holds in his hands
Keeping people captive in shackles and chains
satan is a devil, you see
But if you say Jesus, He will set you free
satan tormented me, both day and night
He had me gripped with fear
I, too, was a captive in shackles and chains
Fear is of the devil, you see
So I said Jesus and He set me free
satan is roaming throughout this land
Gathering people on every hand
But if you say Jesus, He will set you free
Then and only then
Will satan be a captive in shackles and chains

Author, Patricia A. Bayless Behnken
First Pentecostal Church of Murlin Heights
Rev. Ed Ralston, Pastor

His Hand Extended

You may not see your Lord nearby
But you can see my smiling face
You may not feel His tender touch
But my hand o'er your brow you can trace
Your ear may not hear His gentle voice
But my song may comfort your soul
His healing power you may long to feel
And we pray together that He make you whole
Lord, let us be your hand extended
To show your love, mercy and grace
Though others may not see through natural eyes
Let us be a reflection of your lovely face

With Jesus, Never Alone

Sometimes life seems hard, Lord
The things we must go through
Sometime we wonder why, paths lead where they do
Sometimes our feeble legs bend beneath the load they carry
Our hearts seem to melt and then we become so weary
But then I think of where you went that day you walked for me
The load you carried, your legs bent
You stumbled and fell for me
I think about the tears you cried
Your heart was broken
I think about the way You died
Your friends had forsaken you
I'll let you help me carry my load
And I will never alone abide
Upon life's very weary road
You'll always be at my side

The Resurrection

T'was long ago in days now past
My Lord was crucified
He hung upon a cruel cross
And in agony He died
The angry crowds had mocked Him
His flesh was torn apart
And on the cross they nailed Him
He died with a broken heart
The blood He shed was shed for me
The pain He bore for me
The cross He carried up the hill
So that I'd one day be free
They placed His body in a tomb
A stone in front they sealed
So none could steal the body
Saying "He's risen as God revealed"
But in three days my Lord arose
In triumph over the grave
To all believing on His Name
Salvation free He gave
This day He sits on God's right hand
A place for me He'll prepare
By grace I'll enter Heaven's gate
And Christ will meet me there

Thanksgiving

T   is for thanking the Lord everyday
H   is for happiness to walk in His way
A   is for answering to His every call
N   is for near to the cross we must fall
K   is for knees where we are when we pray
S   is for seeking the Lord every day
G   is for goodness on us He bestows
I   is the interest in each one He shows

V	is for victory when in us He lives
I	is for infinite joy that He gives
N	is for new birth the gift from above
G	is for growing in His precious love

A Basket Of Gifts

I have not given you a gift, you said
Ah, yes, but you have been my dearest friend
You've given me a smile when I was down
When I was lonely, you stayed around
You didn't forsake me when I felt lost
You gave me your time, not counting the cost
When I felt confused and unable to think
Your help from God's word was a refreshing drink
And just letting me speak all the thoughts of my heart
Caused peace to come and fears to depart
And when there seemed too much to do
Without a thought, you came to the rescue
You jumped right in with pure physical labor
You forgot about you and just thought of your neighbor
Your kindnesses are greater than I can express
You are all so special and have given your best
So you see my friend, I have a basket of gifts
So great and costly and so heavy to lift
With the natural eye, you're unable to see
I thank you for the best gifts you could have given me

Author, Melvin Jackson
Tabernacle Baptist Church
Rev. Donald Thompson, Pastor

An Easter Song

There is a song this time of year
T'is about the risen Savior
It tells of how He died for us
One day upon the cross
The Easter flowers raises their head
Oh, how their fragrance smell
You see, they grew at the front of the cross
What a story they have to tell
As the angel rolled the stone away
Alleluia, come see the place
Where the Lord Jesu lay
For He is not there
He has risen this day
Sing, sing, Alleluia
Lift up your voices and sing His name
To the Heavens above
Jesus, our precious Savior
He gave us all His wonderful love

I Must Not Faint

The shadows of the evening draws dim
The blackness of the sky creeps across the galaxy
Through the Milky Way
Bringing a close to another day
I must not faint but I trust in God's plan
He's got the whole world in His hands
I will not worry, about the day to come
It was not promised to any one
No matter what the task may be
Or how the road to travel for me
I'll push on and on
Till I see the sun rise
Till I see the glory of God shine through
Then I will gain the prize

I must not faint, I won't let go
Jesus promised
He would never, never leave me
For He loves me so

Where Could I Go

Where could I go
What can I hope to be
All things are possible
It is Christ who strengthens me
No matter how dark and difficult the day
The hand of Jesus still guides the way
Where could I go, and where will the pathway lead
Obedience gives the right of way
The courage I will need
The travel is not easy nor the journeys end to see
The Lord has seen tomorrow and that's enough for me

Little Black Boy

Little black boy, where are you going
What do you hope to be
There's many days to fill your dreams
So why not talk to me
Little black boy what makes you so sad
Why does your countenance fall
You can achieve the best, if only you believe
If you plan to carry the ball
Little black boy, don't run away
What are your doubts and fears
There is a way to plan your day
So wipe away your tears
Don't call me boy
I am a man, you see
Just back away and leave me alone

You are an offense to me
Little black boy, this world is a troubled place
You can't survive using guns and knives
Your end results falls away from grace
Just give me your hand, you can be a man
There is a plan to give you liberty

My Mother's Grandfather's Clock

Papa brought a Grandfather clock to our home many years ago
Where the old clock was purchased
I really do not know
It never made the sounds a clock should make
Hanging on the hallway wall
For attention sake, I guess
Such a mysterious old clock to behold
If it could tick or talk, time consuming stories could be told
Telling tales of a master-clock makers precision work
Proud to say
How it once gave the hour, minutes and seconds of the day
And there now hanging silently bland
No movement of the hour or second hand
Bold faced, stout hearted proud it once was
Giving the time and service for quite a few years
Then one day it finally gave out
Without a whine, whimper or even a shout
It wound up and ran down for the very last time
Lord know what happen, now it will not wind
And then one day as the years passed to and fro
It caught my wife's attention, her eyes all aglow
Such a mysterious piece of art captivating and so proud
Each time she asked about it, I would say Mama
"Leave my clock alone"
Mama lived a mighty long time
Giving service like that old clock
But quite the same as that old clock, her parts worn out
And finally they, too, had to stop
That old clock we brought to our house to pamper and to view

No parts available to make it run like new
Now silently it would hang again, over the fireplace
Standing tall among the few
Striped of paint and varnish, cleaned through and through
Although no parts available for that old clock
However, not the same for Mama
For in Beulah Land, new parts obtained
And there's plenty for me and you

Author, Andrea Attaway Young
Wayman Methodist Church
Rev. Wilbur Lowe, Pastor

Dear God

Dear God, I thank you for my problems
For they draw me to Thee in prayer
Thank you for all of my burdens
You know just how much I can bear
Thank you God, for friends who deceive me
'Cause it shows me the ones who care
I thank you God for the altar
For I can leave all my burdens there

Gonna Make It Despite The Hassles

Gonna make it despite the hassles
That keep easin' up in my face
Gonna finish with flying colors
And set records with my pace
Gonna do it 'cause Jesus loves me
For He came and told me so
One night when I had given up
And had no where to go
Gonna love those who have hurt me
And help others on my way
To learn much more about God's grace
And what it means to pray

Just A Suggestion

When you look into the mirror, and you see nothing at all
When success, or what appears to be, is blocked out, by the wall
When it doesn't seem to matter, that self sees self eye to eye
Just go light, a golden candle, watch it dance, then watch it cry
For it knows the fast explosion, heat and motion in one space
And it knows the depth of fire
True desire face to face
But all the beauty in this moment, lends no reason as to why
That same candle, as it dances and flickers till it starts to cry

Try to discipline emotion
Witness everything in sight
For this candle never fails, to keep it's pledge of giving light
Though it may alter, slightly fading
As the wax begins to fall
It suggests that perseverance, makes a difference after all

It's Alright

Well, it is alright when my last friend turns away, from me
And it's alright
When all lights are out and I can't see a thing
My God knows just what I need
When He comes to touch my soul
When He comes to set me free
And it's alright
Just know that it's alright with me
Well, it's alright
When you say those things that just aren't true
And it's alright
When there's nothing else that I can do
Cause my God will know my heart
And He'll always do His part
When He comes to set me free
And it's alright
Just know that it's alright with me
Well, it's alright
When my last few days on earth are gone
And it's alright
If I never see another dawn
Cause my God will take me up high
Past the sun, the moon and sky
When he comes to set me free
And it's alright
Just know that it's alright with me

Before I Stumble In The Dark

I ask God for understanding
Knowledge followed with patience
So if my scope and phrase appears
Confronted by an inner vioce
The truth shall edify my soul, for God is high and in control
And if allowed just one remark, before I stumble in the dark
I will give thanks for life and love, for Jesus Christ who rose above
All earthly selfishness and greed
He died that He might intercede
For those still lost to death and sin
The battle no one here could win
If I might add to that remarks, before I stumble in the dark
I will confess, and then repent, I'll pray my days be better spent
Teaching what I have come to know, invigorated by the flow
Of being washed in Jesus' blood, the joy of God's eternal flood
And when I find that I've grown weak and it takes all my strength
To speak, then I shall whisper words of prayer
I will ask God to help me bear, life's trials
Trials that make me strong
I will worship Him in song
But when it's time for me to rest
Gods knows I have done my best
If I should let your hand go free, don't panic, my love,
God is with me

Author, Lena Arnold
Revival Center Ministeries
Rev. Willie Mitchell, Pastor

Strokes

You know
God Could have painted
The world
In Only
Black
And
White
But He didn't
Maybe
By His
STROKES
He's
Trying
To tell you something

God's Plan

Desolate, barren, distraught, this I surmise
This is the world I see today
Right before my eyes
Compromised by temptation living day to day
The landlord wants his money
Bills we got to pay
Torn between racism, violent, unruly acts
Dare to kill one another
Yes, that's a fact
The schizophrenic laughs and cries
Won't you dare to help
Put him in a straight jacket
Beat him and leave whelps
The news is filled with crime, people are a mess
Obtain an education
Put crime to a rest
Make the world a better place
Lend a helping hand

Let's get the world together
God's plan

If They Could See Me Now

I imagine that at the moment you opened your eyes
You saw His face
You buried yourself into the crook of His shoulder
You held Him tight and wept
Because you remembered that at one time
You did not believe that He was real
Then He held your face, looked into your eyes, and said
"Don't cry my child
This is not a place for sorrow, but joy
Then at that moment, He gave me a chance to leave heaven
And go back to earth for a while or stay with Him, forever
Then you looked around in awe
At everything your eyes could see
The streets of gold
Shining like transparent glass
The water clear as crystal
The tree of life, majestic and glorious
Then a quick thought
Sudden indecision
As you thought about your family weeping below
He squeezed your hand and said "They will be okay"
As you looked into the face of the almighty, the Savior
Jesus the Messiah, the one in whom you once did not believe in
You knew there was really only one choice, so you chose, life
Everlasting, eternal life
Then secretly you thought
If only they could see me now, they wouldn't cry
So now, I pray that they will all be ready
When He comes for them

Author, Linda Shaw
Shiloh Baptist church
Rev. Henry L. Parker, Pastor

The Savior's Wonderful Gift

The Lord has done great things for me
Opened up my eyes that I could see
All the beauty His hands hath made
In the earth and upon every living man
God's true love for us is what
He did upon the cross
He lived, died and rose again
For this we have Him as
Our Lord and trusted friend

Thank You Lord

Thank you Lord for opening up my eyes
That I may see what it is I am to do or be
God's plan in my life today is with such love
Bestowed upon me in everyway
I know for some special cause I am who I am with flaws
But God's grace and love are within me now
And I cannot explain how
All that I know is it gives me sweet peace
Every lasting joy and rich relief

My Meditation Prayer

Lord, watch over me this day, as I walk along life's way
Keep me centered in your love
And forgive me of what I may be guilty of
I love to be in your care
It helps me have compassion and share
I feel the need to give more genuine love
What I have been so deprived of
I pray today you will guide me in all your ways
I know you will turn my darkest night
Into a wonderful and glorious day

Author, Wealtha Yarbrough
Ethan Temple S.D.A. Church
Rev. Fredrick Russell, Pastor

A Painter's Wish

If I could add some color, to other peoples lives
I'd wipe away their blues and grays, and aid them in their strife
I would paint that hungry stomach, full of food and drink
The hunger pangs would disappear, with the color pink
The naked man would feel my brush, as I clothed him day by day
Protecting him from heat and cold so life won't feel so gray
I'd color in some sunshine, with hues of gold and red
Then when all was said and done
I'd tell him of Jesus and His love
The homeless soul who roams the streets
No where to lay his head
He needs my paintings to guide his feet, before he is quite dead
Some are sick, all bogged down, their body wracked with pain
I'll dip my brush into the paint until they're well again
Colors bold and colors bright, would fill the world with love
And I would thank my Father for the spectrum from above
Down-trodden, heavy-laden, sin-sick souls I see
I'll use the saving blend of paints to relieve and set men free
I'd paint prosperity down the street
Where poor men walk each day
So that they might have their hearts desires and live a better way
The lonely souls who need a friend, and are deeply in despair
I'll paint a path right to his door, and all my time I'd share
If I could mend those broken hearts by painting as I go
The many colors from my brush would never cease to flow
And if by chance each stroke I took, would rid the world of sin
I'd paint each heart so full of love, so Christ could enter in
The magic colors that I have mixed, would soon fill every palette
And then the Angels everywhere would surely sing about it
No more miseries, no more woes, the painting is complete
I'll put away my artist tools for sin has met defeat
Of all the painting on display, in halls throughout the land
The Masterpiece fulfilling God's commands would be mine
The love I'd show to those in need, reflects my love for God
So may I paint a rainbow, as through the world I trod
The many beautiful colors will give a brighter view
And I will keep on painting, till Jesus comes for me

What The New Year Means To Me

Another New Year is here for us, untouched, and oh so new
Another year the Lord has sent
The future is now in view
What do I see for this new Year, what lies in days ahead
The future's not a secret
If the Bible you have read
The New Year that's here, means much to me
In oh' so many ways
If only peace and happiness could rule the coming days
satans busy, working hard, to make us lose our soul
Christ is busy, calling sinners
To free us and make us whole
A New Year means that sin will grow and ever rampant be
No end in sight for the wickedness
As far as man can see
A New Year means that I have time, to do what my Lord has ask
I only want to please Him, by doing His holy will
It means I'll be more loving and giving of my time
And winning souls for Heaven, as on this road I climb
This New Year, I must be strong
For satan's on the prowl
I'll spend more time in prayer, with Him
And I'll begin that now
I thank the Lord for this New Year
It means so much to me
 For it's one more year, He's given me
To put my trust in Him

Author, Howard Ross
Trinity Presbyterian Church
Rev. James Davis, Pastor

Only As

Only as hard as you try
Can you know
Only as far as you want
Can you go
Only as deep as you look
Can you see
Only as great as your faith
Can you be

You Can't Just Be

My mind rushed back to that morning at Lake Geneserat
When the Lord mightily showed me who He was
I was convinced the Master knew all about salvation
And what we needed to do to receive it
But I wasn't so sure He knew how to fish
We had toiled all night, and taken nothing
Then the Master came along, with other thoughts about fishin
He told Peter to throw the net out a little from the land
Out into the deep for a catch
Peter too kinda passed it off, but the Master persisted
Then I heard Peter say
"At your word, Lord, I'm throwin' out the net
We started pulling..and pulling..and pulling
Must 'a been hundreds...thousands of fish
We called our partners to help.. We filled the ship up
But still 'mo fish everywhere
Then we filled their ship..no room left for nothin'
We were beaten and worn out from all the work
Then the ship started sinking from all the fish
I was astounded..just plain scared..thought I would surely die
That moment..that moment..
I knew the Lord was the Son of God..
No' ifs, ands, or buts' about it
All knowing.. all power in his hands

We saw the power.. we saw it
If you could just see what we saw
You couldn't keep on doing what' your doing
You can't just let making a living.. be the only thing
You can't just let having a good time
Be the greatest thing on earth
You can't just be standin' for nothin
You can't just be
We left our nets, and followed Him

Author, William Diggs
Canaan Baptist Church
Rev. Joseph Coleman, Pastor

It Is God And Not We Ourselves

It is God who has created the whole world
And not we ourselves
It is God who has created us and not we ourselves
It is God who has the power to overcome
Death and give life everlasting
And not we ourselves
It is God who has the answer to solve
All our problems and not we ourselves

Judge Not

God has not given any of us
The power to look inside of another
Therefore evaluating a person
Can only be accomplised through
What they do and what they utter
And many of us are good at manipulating these things
So that nothing is actually like it seems
Therefore, judging should be reserved
For God who sees the inside
And knows what the outside means

Formality

People ask me how I'm doing
But they don't really care
It's really just a formality
With meaning, thin as air
Some folks ask me how's your Mom
But they don't wait till I respond
It makes me wonder, if they really care
Or are they just throwing, words out there
They really don't know, if she's alive or dead
Just a formality, void of care
Oh Lord I pray that I have learned one lesson from all this
Help me never to ask empty questions
And to really listen, when people speak
For what a waste of words and time
For the sake of conversation
Help me to treasure honesty and keep it in my heart
If I'm not truly interested
Formality, I won't start

Olivia Harris
Dayton, Ohio

Roots

Roots
Deep in me
Heredity
From people now above
Culture
Makes up my heritage
Relatives
Set situations up to deal with
Genes
Set my ways into action
And kin
Influence me in ways I don't even know

Bernadette Harawa
Dayton, Ohio

A Child Of The Times

Daddy is gone and Mama's gone too
So run, baby run
Get up in the morning, no mom or dad
And no breakfast to eat
No one who seems to care, but to school you must go
School is out, it's time to go home
But there are no loving arms, waiting on you
'Cause nobody is home
So run, baby run
Clothes are needed, but there are none
Still you must dress and still you must go
So run, baby, run
Your life was doomed, before you were born
By someone's addiction, to a thing called dope
That they thought, would not harm you
So run, baby run
With no where to run, and no where to hide
You ran to the school
Where people are waiting, with warm loving arms
And smiling faces
So run, baby run

Annie Turner
Dayton, Ohio

Christ Ambassador Course

The Christ Ambassador course
Has a very specific goal
It equips the saints to teach God's word
In hope of saving souls
When I enrolled in it
I was full of enthusiasm and zeal
But soon after, I realized
That satan was really real
For my schedule was so hectic
And I felt like giving up
That's when I learned, to always keep the Cross
In my pocket
One other thing I learned
That many do not know
Once we're equipped with the word of God
It's up to us to sow the word of God

Sarah Tims
Dayton, Ohio

Express Yourself

We have a right to express ourselves
With body language or maybe words
I choose to write these messages
This is the way I want to be heard
Nobody knows your thoughts but God
He knows just what you think
I want you to hear my thinking
That is why I write my thoughts in ink

Gloria White
Dayton, Ohio

When My Momma Was A Girl

I was round my house a cleaning
When some thoughts gave me a twirl, I thought, I wondered
What my Momma was like, when she was just a girl
Says she from the country, Says things like
"I swanny" and "d'you reckon"
I bet I wouldn't mind being just like her
No, not for a second
I jes know her Momma had a time and made her poor head swirl
Trying to teach my Momma to be a little girl
Bet she went round pranc'in and trying to look cute
And kicking up her heels at church, and then at church to boot
Why I jes' know her po'ol Momma wore her knees out pray'in
And moaning
When she had to face that lil' gal, every single morning
Now I wasn't that much trouble, I was good, kind and sweet
Why, the only thing I might have done
Was to keep things from being, just a little neat
Now when she got a little older and was giving lil' boys the eye
Her Momma, had to drop down on her knees
With just a weak ol sigh
"Lord how could you give me this little girl so sweet,
Then make me have to fast all seven days a week"
But I spect my Grandma was glad, she didn't have a boy '
Cause outside of all those spankings, she was a perfect joy
Have you ever took sometime and thought about yo' Ma
Just what she must ta been like fore she met yo Pa
Good thing he don't know nothin' bout her as a little girl
It's good enough for him to think of her, as his own special pearl

Folk say I look just like my Momma, but I don't really mind
I'd rather look just like her, than these updated kind
And when I think about it, I don't mind what they say
Cause I know just what I'll look like, when I get old and gray
Sometime I look in the mirror and see she's so much dearer
I wonder if my future, will reflect her past
There's so many unasked questions, I'd really like to ask
But I don't set and wonder,
of all the folk packed in this old world
I just wonder what my Mamma was like
When she just a little girl

Rose Wilson
Dayton, Ohio

A Dwelling Place

I shall find my dwelling place in you
All my cares are put upon Thee
No one else loves me the way you do
A dwelling place
A place where the wind blows and whispers my name
Where the rush of water produces a beautiful hymn of praise
A place where the birds fly
In a sky covered with a magnificent rainbow
And the rocks cry out to Thee
The dwelling place
Oh how I yearn to be there now
Nothing for me to worry about
Just surrounded by an abundance of love
Let my heart be annointed
Let me be a light for the unsaved
Let me be a part of your dwelling place

Marisha Lewis
Dayton, Ohio

Who Was That Man

I came down from above
Just to be with you
But you failed, to recognize me
When you saw me, you failed to acknowledge me
I came down from above, my brethren
Just to be with you
You criticize me
Then you turned around and slandered my name
You did everything in your power
Trying to bring me down
When you laughed at the beggar
It was me
That man on the street
With no shoes on his feet
It was me
You gave me no food
Not even a small cup of water, when I was thirty
Because of this you have offended me
Now depart from me, I know you not

Ralph Washington
Dayton, Ohio

A Love Supreme

I will do all I can to be worthy of thee, O' Lord
All praise be to God, to whom all praise is due
God is worthy of the highest praise
God is so good
What a love supreme
God is most compassionate and ever merciful
God is so beautiful
What a love supreme
Blessed be His name
Seek Him everyday
In all ways, seek Him and obey the Lord
For obedience is the highest sacrifice
No road is an easy one
But they all go back to God
There is no one greater than God
All praise be to God
He is truly a love supreme

Julian M. James
Dayton, Ohio

Motherhood

Six pairs of eyes needed, to keep me out of trouble
I can still hear you yelling "Come hear on the double"
With posters on the walls and my head up in the clouds
And you telling me non-stop, to turn that music down
And not to play that music so loud
I know I caused you grief
But through it all, I've learned
It's your love and trust
I hope I've earned
Now, I have two of my own, to turn my hair gray
And now I realize
Just how much you care for me

I Love You Mom!

JoAnna Horning
Columbus, Ohio

My Husband

I sat here on your grave and grieve
For the life we had before
For the husband I have lost
For the husband I adore
There is an ache within my heart
That never goes away
The emptiness and loneliness are here with me today
We met when we were young and our hearts become as one
We were in love from the start and vowed we would never part
We had a full and contented life
And I was proud to be your wife
You were my best friend and the love of my life
And their could never be another, in this world to take your place
My tears, I try to hid, from all others in view
But my tears will never cease, until my life is through
My heart and soul went with you, on the very day you died
And I pray I can be with you, by your side real soon
I sit on your grave and grieve
For the life we had before
For the husband I have lost
For the husband that I adore and love

Alberta Pistoria
Centerville, Ohio

Protrait Of A Grandfather

As I reminisce, I can clearly see
How a Grandfather is supposed to be
Loving, jolly, gay, and fat
Happily as a tot on his knee, I sat
He was pure of heart, with his pipe in his hand
My Grandfather, indeed a good man
Remembering him sitting up in the wee hours of the morning
His peach tree, the willow tree, the broken grapevine
Always joyous at early morn
Whistling and humming, as I popped corn
As time passed and I grew older
His heart grew purer, his generousity bolder
Gandma's biscuits for our Sunday breakfast
Why couldn't these precious moments forever last
His tattered brown sweater, elbows torn
No finer man was ever born
Grandfather eating sharp, longhorn cheese
Grandfather forever attempting to please
Grandfather sitting in his T.V. chair
Now, I look and he's not there
No longer tales of the old South, I'll hear
No longer will he be near
As sure as the sun is in the sky
Good men live , good men die
As my sad eyes gaze into space,
I see a portrait of his kind face
Lamentful and trembling, I raise up my head
And may it be graced by no better man
Dear God, I know there'll never be
No better man, than my grandfather

Joanne Murphy-Gay
Dayton, Ohio

Similarities

We have beautiful flowers
And beautiful trees
As so the story goes
There was a big Oak tree, and there was a small Elm tree
The Oak tree was saying, how he could furnish lumber
For building new homes
The little Spruce tree heard the conversation
Between the two
Big Elm tree bragged, about the great things he could do
The Elm tree told of his big beauitful leaves
The small Spruce tree felt sad
Because the small way it had to please and help mankind
But an idea came to the little Spruce tree
And it said "I ain't small", I can do great things
I can be decorated for the homes
I can make every one happy on Christmas day
I stay green all year round, I have an extensive life
So if you were a tree, which tree would you like to be
The choice is yours to make, but one thing to remember
If you can't be the Sun, be a Star
If you can't be a Star, be the best of whatever you are
For I'm sure of this one thing
We all can be a servant for the Lord

Iula Adams
Dayton, Ohio

Help Someone Today

Have you helped someone today
Have you driven dark clouds away
Did someone burdens you share, to show them that you care
Have you helped someone today
Have you lightened the load of sorrow
From a troubled and weary mind
Have you shown the down-trodden, an easier path to travel
Have you helped someone today
In life there are opportunities to be good and to be kind
Obey God, honor and serve Him
Fulfill whatever your promise
Help someone today
There maybe death or sickness, perhaps a love that was lost
Did you encourage or strengthen
Or aid in paying the cost
Have you helped someone today

In Memory Of
Author, Shadrich J. Liggins
Dayton, Ohio

The Liberator

When it seems the weight of the world is on your shoulders
Give it to the one who carries you and the weight of the world
When life's problems come your way
Give them to Jesus, He will solve them
There is nothing too hard for God
"In all your ways acknowledge Him and He will direct your path"
Spiritual things cannot be proven in laboratories
Or under microscopes
 It's all about Faith and Belief in God
They are about the super-natural
Spiritual things are proven or seem in the transformed lives
And minds of individuals
Persons who have not accepted Jesus whole-heartedly
Cannot discern or speak wisely on spiritual things
When studying your Bible
Ask the Holy Spirit to teach you and guide you
To the truth and understanding of God's word
The whole concept of Christianity is love
God gave His Son Jesus
As a gift to you "John 3:16
Reciprocate, give yourself to Him
Independence day comes for you
The day you accept Jesus in your heart

I Give You Jesus!

Willa D. Little
Dayton, Ohio

A Home Without A Bible

A home without a Bible
Is like a ship without a rudder
If you don't know much about ships
It's like bread without butter
A home without God's word
Is like a child that is lost
Until he hears God's voice
This child's heart cannot rejoice
If you have a Bible
Read it every day
God will bless your home
And He will come to stay
Faith, Hope, and Love
Will be His gift to you
So listen and believe
For God's promises are true

Hazel Quast
Centerville, Ohio

The Heaven Bound Ride

There is a person, so dear to me
That only the depth of love, can God see
Together, both happiness and heartaches we shared
After many long years, I realized how much she really cared
I'll never again, find a friend quiet so true
One I can turn too, when lonely and blue
As I lie here tonight, tears sting my eyes
For I realize we've said, our final good-byes
Today, I laid my dear Mother to rest, in a cold box of grey
My heart is so burdened, no words can I say
But my heart swells so greatly, with joy and with pride
For a golden coach is waiting, to take my Mother
For that Heaven-Bound Ride

Joyce Fullen
Xenia, Ohio

Reunion

She met me at the airport with a red rose
My daughter of twenty-six years
Known to be but two days
When I signed the papers
The agency told me that I would never see her again
But she found me through Divine Agency
Her smile is curiously familiar
And from her lips, a soft breathless cry
"Alice"
"Connie"
A hug across the years
A touch to heal the loss
"Is it really you"
I can't stop staring at her face
She has her father's blue eyes
My cheekbones
My curling baby toe
We stayed awake til four a.m.
Damp tissues in our laps
She sparkles, a gem in the sand of time
Uncovered by a wave of grace
And for a moment all stands still
Strange providence gives back this child
Lost piece in my heart's puzzle
And the picture is now complete
With a rose, a daughter's kiss
And those curling little toes

Alice C. Linsley
Sidney, Ohio

The Light

I am the light to lead the way
I shine in darkness and it flees away
I am a light for you, if you will trust and obey
Darkness must flee when I come on the scene
Just trust in me, I will give you liberty
Light shines brightly each and every day
Light shines brightly and scares the demons away
Light shines brightly in the spirit of man
The light is shining so let's say Amen!

Virginia Wood
Columbus, Ohio

Teenage Years

You're thirteen now, a young lady
An age when the world around you comes alive
And with relief you sigh, teenage years
Have finally arrived
Growing up isn't easy or always a lot of fun
It requires patience and years to get the job done
These years you're entering are special years
So be wise, fill them with happiness not tears
Use these years to get to know yourself
God made us each different than anyone else
What I'm trying to say with these few lines
Is that I love you and think you're growing up fine

Joyce Miller
Sidney, Ohio

Follower of Christ

As a follower of Christ it gets, hard some times
And you feel that you have no where to turn to
He said in His word, I will never leave you alone
And inside your soul His spirits burns
We live in a world where darkness is called night
But day does not always mean seeing the light
We question ourselves about our actions
Steady, fighting to win the spiritual fight
People can only make you laugh
And for a while put your mind at ease
But God can calm the raging waters
And part the untamed seas
As followers of Christ, we have to stand tall
And hold on to His unchanging hand
Praise His name and live by the sword
And He will lead you into His promised land

Kellie Fair
Middletown, Ohio

Where

As I lie in my bed, in the stillness of the night
I can't help but to think
Lord, you are no where in sight
Frustration, hurt and so much pain
What's in this life for me to gain
I take a deep breath and then a sigh
And in no time at all, I ask the question, why
I have tried so hard to do my best
To do all that is right
But it seems that I am always, entering a test
There is so much that I don't understand
Lord, where is your helping hand
As I lie in my bed and I shed tears
I am reminded that Jesus is with me
There is no reason to fear
He is my Savior and my friend
My questions He will answer
My dreams will become true
If only on Him I completely depend

Georgetta Von Dolln
Grove City, Ohio

Good-Bye My Friend

Good-bye my friend, you will be missed
God had a plan for you
Good-bye my friend, the late talks at night will be no more
Good-bye my friend your work here is done
Your work in heaven has just begun
There will be no more misunderstanding there
The Lord will say stand at the door
And let them come in
No more tears, no more sorrow, no more good byes
You have a mansion that's been prepared for you
You can walk to the street of gold
Entering that mansion, so bright and fair
You can sing His praises and lift a hymn or two
You're gone, but never will you be forgotten
The things you have done, have left a mark in time
You will be missed, but never forgotten
Good-bye my friend

Lollie Brooks
Massillon, Ohio

Thankful For Haves

I have stood at eternity's door and I was not afraid
For death is an entry, to endless pleasures there
Because I am God's child, I have felt the brush of Angel-wings
As I neared, God's throne in prayer
I have been immersed in His holy love
The holy ghost comforted me
I have discerned God's majesty, in the flash of lighting
And I have remembered His promise
In the spectrum of the rainbow
I have perceived His law of nature
When the spring was pink of dogwood trees
And change to scarlet coats for Autumn
I have breathed the odor of Eden, in the fragrance of lilac blooms
I have seen the proof of God's creation
In uniquely designed snowflakes
I have soared through misty clouds
Above mountain heights and ocean depths
Trusting in God's law of gravity
I have flown through stormy turbulence of a Pacific typhoon
And watched God open a sunhole
As he reached maximum altitude
I have deciphered maternal love
Through my mother's Godly devotion
I have erased fears of nonentity, in the birth of my child
I have sensed a Heavenly host, saying "Amen"
To my Father's humble prayers
I have made an altar in the desert
And found God amid the cactus
I have communed with Him in silence
When pain negated vocal pleas
I have felt His healing of spirit and of body
By His blessed, "Be at peace my child"
I have ten thousand "haves" to be thankful for
I've been thanking God, for everyone of them

Billie L. King
Sidney, Ohio

Life

Life is too short to be about hate, fear, guilt, worry or doubt
We know not the day, moment or hour, death may appear
With all of it's power
To take life from the innocent,
and from ones we hold so dear
Death is so near
Within our hearts, our minds and our souls
Death takes it's monumental toil
How we truly feel, those dead will never know
It is so important
To let positive loving feelings now show
Life is but one moment, in time
Death is an eternity
And cannot be comprehended, by the average mind
It may be damnation or an everlasting hell
It maybe as the Bible foretells
For those whose lives have turned right and gone straight
There may truly be the pearly gates
Streets of pure gold, mansions in the sky, joy, peace and love
Where good never dies
Whether one believes or not
What matters is what your life is about
What comes from within your heart
The deeds you have done and the seeds you have sown
Knowing we never live alone
We touch and we are touched, with each moment of life
We each must live in the now
Make it worth the living
Someway, somehow
Life is too short to be about pain, misery, hate or doubt
Live each moment as though it's your last
Yesterday only belongs in the past

Vera Thomas
Canton, Ohio

It Was Me

When your broken heart was mended
And your sickness finally ended
And when in need, you were befriended
It was me
When you thought you couldn't take it
And to smile, you had to fake it
But you found the strength to make it
It was me
When the situation tried you
And your friends all denied you
Yet you felt someone beside you
It was me
When you made the right decision
With perfect timing and precision
Because you somehow had a vision
It was me
When the storm left you battered
And your hopes and dreams were shattered
But someone made you feel like life really mattered
It was me
And after years of hesitation
You had the urge to seek salvation
Well, for your information
It was me

R. A. Cooper
Lorain, Ohio

We Have A Savior

We have a Savior, He's always there
Confess Him, them address Him as your Lord
The Prince of Peace
Your wheel in the middle of a wheel
Your life will become, better
More meaningful and real
He comes to save and He will save you
When life depraves you
He will be there to assist you
When life dimisses you
Oh' He will take care of your every need
Just let Him lead you
And if you follow, and keep your eyes
And your mind on Him
And let Him take command
Your life will be sweeter
Amen, Amen, Amen!!!

James E. Nesbitt
Columbus, Ohio

God Has A Way

His ways are not ours and His timing is His own
He directs and He leads
Our destiny, only through Him is known
Yes, God has a way and I'm so glad
Because His way is the best way
I'm telling you the truth and I have the proof
He said that He would never leave you
Has He ever left you alone?
No, my friend!
 He's always there everytime to take you in
When times seem discouraging
And the going gets rough
We have the assurance
That God is enough
Because He has a way
And He's right on time, everyday
He'll keep you
He gives us all we need
And my friend, that's guaranteed
Because your Maker loves you
He made you in His image, you see
And we must trust and obey
Even when we can't see our way
Won't you open your heart today
Listen to what God has to say
Let Him in your heart, to stay
He'll make everything allright
Because God, our Father has away

James E. Nesbitt
Columbus, Ohio

Denomination

It doesn't matter what denomination you are
As long as God is there
As long as the Holy Spirit in you abide
You and the Lord can share
My Bible says, "Repent, Believe and be Baptized
These things in Jesus name".
The Holy Spirit
Will ascend upon you
And receive your life again
What does it matter if you say
I'm Presbyterian, Baptist, Catholic, Holiness or such
The thing that really makes the difference
Are you and God in Touch
One God-One Spirit-One-Faith
That keeps us all
The name means nothing less
And when we depart from this great Earth
There's no denomination on our chest
We all live and die miraculously
Just like the miracle of giving birth
We come here with no denomination
And we'll leave this world as such
So don't let this word, denominations confuse you
For in the book I read
"The Son of Man will claim His own"
 He'll know you by your deeds".

Nealor Green
Columbus, Ohio

A Godly Mother

The word of God is a lamp unto her feet
This is seen by everyone she meets
Prayer is her backbone
This is how she remains strong
Love, it's a must
For God is in whom she trusts
Faith, she wears it like a lovely gown
One day she will receive her golden crown
For she is a Godly Mother!

Mary McKnight
Columbus, Ohio

My Mother

A pillar of strength
On her knees she bent to pray to God for a blessing
Mother always took care of me
Made me feel better when I scraped a knee
Took me to Sunday school
So I would learn of God and have a fire in my heart
That would burn forever for Him
There I learned to treat people with kindness and respect
I learned to love myself and have self respect for others
To Challenge those that challenge me
To take hold of the breast plate of armor and gird my loins
For out here in this world
Mother told me as she lay dying
Be ever watchful and stay with God
For He will calm the raging storms
He will use His rod against those that harm you
He will also, chastise, those that do not obey Him
He does everything out of Love
Call on Him any time you need Him
He will be there in your time of need

Elaine Saffold
Dayton, Ohio

How To Love Yourself

Each day you rise up
You must confront the greatness inside of you
You are a warm and genuine, Afrikan spirit
But that is just one clue
Always give your life the best that you've got
It's for you and no one else
The most important person to be in life, will always be yourself
Forget your height, your size, your might
Your ego, and your strength
Take a serious look at the attitude you have
It's direction, and it's length
This love that you have for people you meet
It really comes from the heart
Just change its direction toward yourself
You have truly an awesome start
You will make mistakes, don't think it's because
You really are no good
God's mightest men, call it honor, you see
To stand where they once stood
There is no reason to hide, deep down inside
Something you truly feel
Life will take you up, then it will bring you down
So just try and stay for real
How to succeed at loving yourself
I can humbly offer this small clue
All that you say and all that you feel
Should be mirrored in what you do!

Donald E. Law
Columbus , Ohio

Revelation in Prayer

I have loved thee with an everlasting love
I have healed thee, believe it
I will see you thru
Be still and know that I am God
Fret not thy self because of the evil doer
Be not afraid
Peace, happiness are yours
Be not weary in well doing
Give of your substance
God measure pressdown
I will give unto your bosom
Mine eyes will follow you everywhere you go
I will protect you

Annie M. King
Dayton, Ohio

To order additional copies of

Anthology of Ohio Poets

please send $10.00 and $3.00
shipping and handling to:

Tina Toles
P. O. Box 7403
Dayton, Ohio 45407
937-832-0541